Maid of Honor Handbook: The Duties, Details, and Delights

By
Melinda Meier

Table of Contents

Thank you to my Family, Friends and God.

Thanks to Jen, Theresa, Heather and Katie
For inspiration and support

Introduction

Your best friend, sister, cousin, college roommate, or someone else special in your life has asked you to be the Maid or Matron of Honor at her wedding. Congratulations! As the title implies, it is a great honor to be asked to be the Maid of Honor at a wedding. One bride I talked to had this to say about her sister and Maid of Honor:

"The most special part of her being my maid of honor was that she was my sister. This made the event and her role even more memorable and blessed to me. It was indeed my honor to have her by my side during the ceremony".

Brides regard the Maid of Honor as a cherished friend, ultimate confidant, trusted companion, and true supporter.

You might be asking, though, what exactly does being a Maid of Honor mean? What am I expected to do as the Maid of Honor?

You've come to the right place. In this book, you will learn what your duties are, creative ideas for making the details special, and how to deal with the nervous bride. Being a Maid of Honor is a lot of work, but with some organization, guidance, and flexibility, it is also a lot of fun. You will be spending a lot of time with the bride, and will likely strengthen your relationship even more.

Let's get started and learn what you need to know to be the best maid of Honor ever!

Chapter 1   Wedding Plans

First, get the bride organized. This comes naturally to some people and not to others. She will need some sort of portable filing system. (such as an accordian file or 3 ring binder with plastic inserts).

The tags should hold titles like:

-Ceremony

-Reception

-Gown

-Bridesmaid Dresses

-Tuxedos

-Flowers/Centerpieces

-DJ/Band

-Photographer

-Seating Charts/Placecards

This allows for her to be able to save ideas, magazine clippings, or receipts. Also, she should always be carrying a wedding designated notebook with her for jotting down ideas, phone numbers, vendors, etc.

Next, the bride will need to think about securing facilities for the ceremony and reception. In order to be able to do this, she must also choose when she wants to tie the knot.

How do they choose a date?

Choosing a date is often the first thing a bride and her fiancé do after they become engaged. For some brides, it is an easy decision. Others might not know what factors play into choosing a date.

There are a few things to consider when choosing a date:

1. **What is the bride's favorite season?** If she loves the crisp air of autumn with the brightly colored leaves, try an October or early November date. Does the bride love swirling snow? Has she always wanted a spring wedding? Are her favorite flowers in season during the summer?

2. **What conflicts might the guests face?** If there are several spring graduations in the bride's family, opt for an earlier spring date. Does the bride's father have an out-of-country business meeting every January? Try to accommodate the big conflicts, but make sure the bride doesn't drive herself crazy trying to tailor her date to every potential guests' schedule.

Story Box

Jen married her groom, Mike, on one of the biggest game days in the football season. Rather than trying to fight it, she arranged for a TV to play the game in the bar area of the reception, and the bridal party did their pictures during most of it. All the football fans were happy, and the night went perfectly!

---

3. **What dates are special to the bride and groom?** Some brides choose a date because it is the birthday of a beloved grandparent who has passed away, because it is an anniversary in her relationship with her fiancé, or for some other special reason. Choosing a date with meaning can add even more to an already extraordinary day.

4. **What is the best time of month for the bridal couple?** If the groom has a heavy work load at the end of each month, perhaps the second weekend will be best – he'll have a week to recover from last month's rush, and should be back in time for the next.

5. **When is the bride's dream reception site available?** One common misconception is that the bride must have a date set in stone before she can look for a church and reception site. In actuality, she might have better luck if she can be flexible. Suppose the bride dreams of getting

married at the botanical gardens in spring. She will have more luck finding a springtime date if she can work around other reservations the reception site has made with other brides.

Idea Box

Heather married Steve in mid-December, and she knew people would be planning holiday parties way before the invitations for the wedding went out. So, they made magnets on their home computer with the skyline of Minneapolis (where they got married) and their names and wedding date printed on the bottom. They mailed them out months in advance so their guests would know to hold the day, even without the official invitation!

Ceremony and reception sites

Some brides choose to have the ceremony and reception in the same place. Churches sometimes have party halls or gardens on the premises that are quite beautiful. Other brides might choose to have the ceremony outside of a church at a park or in a reception hall. It can be easier to book one place for both the ceremony and the reception.

However, many brides have separate locations for the ceremony and the reception. In this case, the bride will need to do some extra planning (and maybe leave some more time) to coordinate all the times on the same date.

The best way to advise the bride to approach this is to just pick up the phone and make some calls. She should have in mind which site is her priority. For example, if it is her family's tradition to wed in the church she attended as a child, the bride might first confirm the date with the church, then call several reception sites to see which has availability on that date.

Visiting potential sites

The bride will likely ask you to visit potential ceremony and reception sites with her. Your role should be to talk to her as you tour each site, ask questions she might not think of, and just chat with her about them to help her form her impressions. Visiting many sites can make a bride's head spin! Soon, all the details will run together in her mind and she won't remember what is what.

Keep notes on each site you visit. Keep track of where you and the bride visit, the name of the contact person, the price of rental, hours of availability, capacity, and all the other details the bride will need to know. Also make notes about the positive or negative comments the bride whispers to you as you tour each facility. Use the handy checklist (pages 9-11) and make your notes right there for the bride!

Ceremony Sites: What to look for:

For the ceremony site, take note of the following things:

1. **Capacity** – How many people can the facility seat?

2. **Fee** – How much does it cost to book the facility?

3. **Hours available** – How early can you get into the facility to set-up, get dressed and start pictures?

4. **Restroom facilities** – Are the restrooms clean and well-stocked? Are the restrooms large enough? (A good rule of thumb is one facility for each 40-50 guests) If it is an outdoor site such as a park, do you need to rent portable restrooms?

5. **Staging Area** – Is there an area where the bridal party can line up that is relatively out of sight? How close is the staging area to the restrooms and dressing room?

6. **Dressing Room** – Is there a place where the bride and bridesmaids can dress and do last minute primping? It can be as simple as a classroom, a lounge, or a library.

7. **Parking** – Is there ample parking? Is the sign for the site easy to read? There may even be valet available. Is there a fee for this?

8. **Decoration Style/Colors** – What is the style of the facility? Will you need to dress it up with lots of your own decorations? Do the colors clash with the wedding colors?

9. **Miscellaneous** – Does the site prohibit throwing birdseed or flower petals as the bride and groom emerge after the ceremony? Are there restrictions on decorating?

Reception sites: What to Look for

Take note of the following things when looking at each reception facility:

1. **Capacity** – How many people can the facility seat for dinner, leaving room for a DJ or band, a dance floor, gift table and mingling room? If it is an outdoor facility, is there backup space for bad weather? Do they have pictures of a wedding setup in the space, or can you stop by while a wedding is being setup to scope it out?

2. **Fee** – How much does the facility cost? Is it a flat fee or a per-person fee? How many hours does the fee include? What is the down payment required? Is there a security deposit? When will it be returned?

3. **Hours Available** – Is the facility available at a reasonable time after the ceremony? When are all guests required to leave? Is there an overtime fee if the party lasts longer? Will there be another event in the facility on the same day?

4. **Restroom Facilities** – Are there enough restrooms for all the quests? Is it conveniently located? Is it clean and well-stocked with tissues, hand towels and toilet paper?

5. **Decorations Style/Colors** – What is the style of the facility? Do the style and colors clash with the theme and colors of the wedding? Do they have any restrictions?

6. **Parking** – Is there ample parking available? Is there vallet parking available? Is there a fee for valet parking?

Ceremony Site Checklist

1. **Name of Facility**_____

2. **Contact Person**_____

3. **Contact Information**

    (phone)_____

    (fax)_____

    (email)_____

    (address)_____

    _____

4. **Capacity**_____

5. **Fee**_____

6. **Hours Available**_____

7. **Restroom Facilities**_____

8. **Staging Area**_____

9. **Dressing Room**_____

10. **Parking**_____

11. **Decorating Style/Color**_____

12. **Miscellaneous**_____

Reception Site Checklist

1. **Name of Facility**_____

2. **Contact Person**_____

3. **Contact Information**

    (phone)_____

    (fax)_____

    (email)_____

    (address)_____

4. **Capacity**_____

5. **Fee**_____

6. **Hours Available**_____

7. **Restroom Facilities**_____

8. **Dressing Room**_____

9. **Parking**_____

10. **Onsite Caterer/List of Approved Caterers?**_____

    _____

11. **Alcohol Allowed? Provided by Facility?**_____

12. **Decorating Style/Color**_____

13. Dance Floor?_____

14. Number of outlets?_____

15. Miscellaneous_____

Comments:

Reception Ideas

Is the bride stumped about places to have the reception? Offer these creative suggestions!

Art gallery	Historical building
Beachfront	Inn
Boat	Park
Botanical gardens	Theme park
Farmhouse	Yacht club
Greenhouse	Zoo

Chapter 2   Planning the Shower

Time for the bridal shower!   And just who is responsible for planning and throwing the bridal shower? You guessed it – the Maid of Honor. But don't panic! The bridal shower is supposed to be fun, even for you. Note: It is possible that the bride will be having a separate family shower, girlfriend shower and/or co-worker shower.

The first thing to keep in mind is what the bride's expectations are for the shower. Does she envision a fancy high tea with lots of lace and delicate pastries, or does she prefer a backyard barbeque with beer and gag gifts? Take your cue from the bride. Find out how formal she wants the shower to be, and let that be your ultimate guide.

Ask the bride about her wedding registry. The couple should complete the registry approximately one month before the bridal shower. You can include a card with the invitations stating where to buy gifts off the wedding registry.

The Guest List

Guests at a bridal shower generally include the bride's closest friends and family. What's the difference between the guest list at a shower, a bachelorette party, and the wedding itself, you may ask?

Imagine a pyramid; the closest gals are at the top of the pyramid, and are invited to the bachelorette party. These are best friends and closest family members. It would be acceptable to invite some coworkers but not others, some girlfriends but not all, and just the bride's favorite aunt.

The shower is the middle of the pyramid crowd, and includes all of the females invited to the wedding that the bride is fairly close with. It can include all the aunts, cousins, coworkers, and friends, or just family and close friends. There is a lot of flexibility in the shower guest list. Most of the time, you can get the guest list for the shower from the bride. Some showers, however, are designed to be a surprise party for the bride. In this case, ask the bride's mom or sisters who should be invited.

Etiquette

Not all females invited to the wedding need to be invited to the shower. However, everyone invited to the shower must also be invited to the wedding. Gone are the days of etiquette restricting the bride's mother and sisters' role in planning the shower. Feel free to ask for help from them! If you are inviting out-of-town guests, send invitations in plenty of time so all guests can make travel arrangements.

Etiquette Question

Q: The bride's guest list for the shower includes many people from out of town that she feels she must invite. She doesn't think many will make the trip. We can't decide whether to send them invites because the bride does not want them to feel obligated to send a gift. What should we do?

A: Chances are, all of the out of town invitees will be overjoyed to be included even if they can't make the trip, and can't wait to go shopping so they can send something and be remembered at the shower. Remind the bride that, just like her, everyone is filled with the best of intentions. If she receives a gift from someone unexpected, tell her to graciously accept and know the gift-giver simply wants to share in the joy of the day. If she expects a gift from someone and does not receive one, remind her that wedding etiquette is tricky, and that person surely meant no harm. Weddings are about celebrating the life the bride and groom are about to begin together, and the bride and all of her guests know that gifts are just one way to show happiness.

Themes

Planning the bride's shower around a theme can make it easier to plan and lots of fun. It can be as simple as planning the décor around the bride's favorite color, or as complicated as a destination theme (where is the couple honeymooning?) with native cuisine, traditional dress and décor – the sky is the limit! You might plan a "Months of the Year" shower, where guests are assigned a month of the year to keep in mind when buying a gift. A guest assigned to January might buy a crock-pot for hot meals on cold nights. Those with summer months could select a sexy bathing suit or a barbeque set.

A "Garden shower" would include custom-printed seed packets as the invitations, serve dip from mini-garden pails, and use individual tiny pots of fresh flowers as place cards.

Another idea is a "Room by Room" theme. Each guest can purchase a gift for a specific room in the house.

If you decide to do a theme shower, be creative! Take cues from the bride's interests and passions, and go from there. Above all, have fun with it!

Couples Showers

More and more, people are throwing couples showers, with a coed guest list and, usually, a more casual environment. Most couple showers are held at someone's home or a restaurant, as opposed to a spa or garden. If you and the bride decide on a couples shower, you might ask for planning help from the best man or the other attendants. Bear in mind, there might be football at the couples shower. You are less likely to impress the male guests with handmade decorations or by handcarving the vegetables into bride shapes. If the bride yearns for these kinds of details and female-bonding, perhaps the groomsmen can throw a couples shower, and you, the Maid of Honor, can plan a separate girls-only shower. That said, couples showers are usually uproariously fun. It's the bride's choice!

Shower Sites

The first thing to consider in planning a shower is where it will be held. Many showers can be accommodated in someone's home, which can help cut costs dramatically. If the guest list is very small or very big (and depending on your budget), you might consider hosting the shower at a restaurant, spa, pub, coffee house, or garden.

Story box

Susan's Maid of Honor, Katie, says, "there was a huge blizzard the day before Susan's shower, and almost all of the guests canceled at the last minute. Since we had planned a potluck-style shower, we were left with few guests and not much food! So instead, Susan, her sisters and I (the only remaining guests) headed to the day spa and had ·an afternoon of facials, massages, and giggling. It was fabulous! That spring, we planned a casual couples shower and it was warm enough to barbeque."

Selecting a Shower Date

Once you have the perfect place for the shower lined up, start thinking about a date and time. Weekend days work best for most people, of course, but the time of day depends largely on how complex an affair the bride wants the shower to be. If several guests are flying in from out of town, consider a late-Saturday or early-Sunday shower so they have time to fly in and fly out without taking a day off work. Earlier showers (beginning between 9 and 11AM) are perfect for brunch, tea, mimosas, and pastries, and tend to be slightly more formal.

Afternoon showers, on the other hand, can be casual or more fancy. Showers that begin between 2 and 4PM are perfect for potlucks, barbeques, delicious appetizers, wine bar, coolers full of water, soda, and beer.

Invitations

Time to send the invitations! If any of the guests are from out of town, send the invitations at least a month or so in advance. If everyone is local, a few weeks' notice will be just fine. Guests will use the invitation to get a sense of the level of formality of the shower. Lace-trimmed invites with careful lettering will let your guests know it is more formal.

Consider how you would like guests to RSVP. Set a cut-off date ("Please RSVP by July 1," generally 2 weeks before the shower) so that you have time to shop and prepare for the correct number of guests. Do you want guests to RSVP only if they will not be coming, or do you want all guests to RSVP either way? You could write "RSVP (regrets only please) by July 1". Will you list *your* phone number and/or email address? Make sure whichever phone number you use has voicemail or an answering machine.

Include in the invitation:

1. The bride's name
2. The date, time, and place
3. Who is throwing the shower
4. Where the bride is registered
5. Directions and, for out-of-town guests, phone numbers for nearby hotels. Add a separate piece of paper with directions, address, and phone number in case guests get lost.
6. A way for guests to RSVP or call with questions
7. A sense of whether a full meal will be provided, so guests know whether to eat before they come. Example: "Shower luncheon" or "Brunch celebration" or "Appetizers & Wine will be served".

Fun Fact

Where does the abbreviation "RSVP" come from, you ask? It's short for "répondez s'il vous plaît," which is French for "please reply."

The Menu

What to serve, what to serve... Of course you want to put on a gorgeous and delicious spread, but consider the number of guests and your budget. If you are expecting 15 people, you can do more elaborate things than if the bride insists on inviting 100. If you plan to hire a caterer, ask for samples from a few different caterers. Get referrals from friends. Ask about bulk discounts and ways to cut costs. If you plan to prepare the food yourself, look for sales in the weeks before the shower and freeze anything you can get for a steal!

When planning the menu, first decide whether you will be serving a full meal, or appetizers only. If you plan a full brunch or lunch, plan something that is in line with the formality of the shower. A more formal affair might mean you serve finger sandwiches, crab salad, fancy rolls, steamed vegetables, and punch or champagne from a sparkling punch bowl. Casual shower fare might include hamburgers, grilled chicken, chips, raw veggies, and cans of soda and beer. The same goes for appetizers: a formal shower demands shrimp, fine cheeses and grapes, spinach-filled triangles, and filet mignon bites.

Informal showers can appetize with cold veggies, pigs-in-blankets, chips and dip, and deviled eggs.

Decide what kinds of beverages you will serve. Punch is a shower staple, and there are some delicious recipes. If you decide to serve alcohol, make sure to have plenty of non-alcoholic options available as well. Have at least one diet option for diabetics and the calorie-conscious.

Whatever you decide on for the menu, presentation counts! When arranging trays of food, try to include as many colors as possible on each tray. It doesn't have to be a work of art, but make it appealing.

Decorations

Half the fun of a wedding shower is decorating. If you have a theme for the shower, you probably already have a good idea about what kind of décor will be appropriate. The basics: make sure to cover tables in linens and have a few wedding-themed items hanging about (paper wedding bells, white tulle, etc.). Place cards and favors can add to the décor as well. Centerpieces add elegance to any party, and they can be given away as shower game prizes. Which brings us to…

Shower Games

Shower games are loads of fun, especially when the guests aren't acquainted with one another yet. A great shower game can really break the ice so conversation bubbles throughout the whole shower.

Here are a few ideas to get you started. Do some research and be creative!

1. Shower Bingo – Make bingo cards containing popular shower gift items. As the bride opens the gifts, guests mark off their cards with the corresponding item. Establish what makes a "bingo" upfront (any line, 4 corners, fill the whole card, etc.).

2. What's in your purse? – Make a list of common or not so common things that women carry in their purse. Associate a point value based on uniqueness of items. Example: Fingernail clipper, bobby pin, crayon, two-dollar bill. Be creative.

3. Advice for the Couple – Ask each guest to write down some advice on marriage for the to-be-weds. Provide slips of paper with wedding art on it. Guests can collaborate, which will get them talking. Let the kids join in – it makes for some adorable moments. After the shower, arrange all the papers into an "advice book" for the lovely couple.

4. Newly to be Wed Questions. Call the groom and ask him 10 questions. How does he think the future bride would respond? Example: How many kids do you want? If you could travel anywhere in the world, where would it be? What is your favorite food? (Remember: He needs to

answer the questions as how he thinks his future wife would answer). Ask these same 10 questions of the guests at the shower. Whoever gets the most answers correct – Is the winner. After the guests answer those questions, reveal how the groom answered. It's fun to see how well the couple knows each other!!

Gift Time!

And now, the true essence of the bridal shower: opening gifts! Make sure the bride has plenty of space – those gifts will pile up, and she needs some air. Make sure to have a trash bag handy for wrapping paper.

Part of the fun of opening gifts is the old superstition that every bow the bride breaks represents one child she will bear. Make sure the bride is prepared for this, and play it up! As each gift is opened, thread each ribbon or bow through a hole in a paper plate. This will serve as the faux bouquet during the wedding rehearsal. Or save them and you can make it in your spare time.

The bride will need to know whom each gift is from so her thank-you notes can be detailed. As the bride opens her gifts, make sure you or someone you designate is taking notes. Usually the hostess takes notes, however if you are busy refilling drinks and replenishing food, delegate. Make sure the note-taker writes:

- Who the gift is from
- What the gift is
- Any particularly special words in the card.

After the shower, provide these notes and the address list you used to mail the invitations. The bride will eternally grateful!

Planning a shower is hard work! But, the bride will never forget you for doing such a fabulous job. Remember that the goal of the shower is to have fun. Don't let yourself become overwhelmed with details; it's not worth the fun you'll miss out on!

Planning Checklist:
1. Location of shower?
2. Will you have a full lunch or dinner, or just hors d'oeuvres? Will you have it catered, cook yourself, or ask guests to bring their favorite dish?
3. What will the drinks be? Punch? Tea? Wine and champagne? Beer?
4. Will you plan the shower around a theme?
5. How will guests RSVP?
6. How will you inform guests about where the bride is registered?
7. Who will coordinate the gift-opening, such as seating so guests can see each package being opened, writing down who gave the bride what gift, etc.?

train from the alteration shop. They are absolute experts in bustling gowns and can show you the ins and outs of the bride's particular gown. After the last fitting, the gown is usually steamed, so practice before that happens. If you cannot go with the bride to a fitting, don't fret. The bride will learn how her gown should be bustled during her fittings, and she can probably talk you through it after the ceremony.

Note: If the bride is having a personal attendant at her wedding, discuss with the bride and the personal attendant who will take care specific responsibilities.

Vendors

You should also help the bride confirm delivery times for the flowers, cake, and other items that need to be dropped off at the wedding or reception site. Usually these details will be ironed out in a contract made at the time of the order, but help the bride call about a week in advance to confirm the details. Also make sure to confirm with the wedding and reception site at what time the vendors and wedding party can access the site. There's nothing worse than arriving at the ceremony to begin getting ready, only to be confronted with dark windows and locked doors!

The best way to anticipate what you can do now to make the wedding day so smoothly is to go through the details of what will happen on the wedding day in your mind.

Let's Get Beautiful

First, the bride might have appointments to have her hair, nails, and/or makeup done. Many brides also plan a beauty session at home before the wedding that you will be involved in. Gather any beauty supplies you need about a week before so that if you are running low on anything you have plenty of time to restock.

Of course, every bride wants to look her best on her wedding day. This often involves facials, treatments, and other beauty regimens before the wedding day itself. Remind the bride that it can be dangerous to make drastic changes the month before the wedding. If the bride wants to try a new hair color, for example, encourage her to do it over a month in advance. If the results are fabulous, she can freshen the look just before the wedding.

Wedding Day Troubleshooting

Any bride is bound to need a few things on hand before the ceremony in order to get ready. There is also always the potential for minor beauty and sewing crises just before the wedding. In order to be prepared for last-minute emergencies, gather a kit of supplies in the week before the wedding. You probably have most of this stuff on hand at home. Throw the following items in a bag to take with you to the ceremony.

The "Must Have" Kit:

- A makeup kit for touch-ups (bring your own makeup, and have the bride bring her personal stash)
- Anti-static cling spray
- Hairspray (also works for anti-static, if you run out of it!)
- Breath mints, mouthwash, gum, etc.
- Clear deodorant
- Dental floss
- Emery board
- Hair brush and comb
- Bobby pins
- Perfume
- Linen-freshening spray (beware of moisture spots of silky fabrics though! If you need to get rid of musty or bad smells on silks or satins, turn the garment inside out and spray from a safe distance)
- Pencil and paper (no exploding pens to worry about!)
- A cell phone – if you or the bride don't have one, see if a bridesmaid has one to bring, or if you can borrow one.
- A list of phone numbers, including the officiator, florist, mothers of the bride and groom, reception site, caterer, cake vendor, limo driver, band or DJ, and anyone else responsible for any aspect of the wedding day.
- Safety Pins

- Band-Aids (for blister on feet or to tighten loose shoes)
- Aspirin
- Antacids
- Scissors
- Needle with white and black thread
- Clear Nail Polish
- Sanitary Pads/Tampons
- Wide Scotch Tape (Can hold up a hem if it starts to come out) Also picks up lint, dirt and hair from bride's train

Seem like a lot of stuff? It is, in a way, but you never know exactly what you and the bride will need last minute. Bring sample or travel sizes when possible to save space. You also might want to designate someone who is not in the wedding party to grab your emergency kit after the ceremony, since you will be busy with pictures and details, and probably don't want to make a grand entrance at the reception with a huge gym bag full of goodies.

There are a few other things you might want to keep on hand, as well. These are less likely to be needed than the things in the above list, but if you do need them and they aren't handy, you might find yourself making a mad dash for the nearest store. Not fun. Try keeping the following items in a handy pack that you can keep in the trunk of your car at the wedding. If you need them, you can get them quickly (or better yet, send the bride's cousin who arrived two hours early), but you won't have to haul it inside at the beginning of your day along with the other items, your dress, favors, the flower girl's basket, etc.

The "What-If?" Kit:

- Extra panty hose – bring several pairs; for the bride (get her size!), and also bridesmaids
- Nail polish in the colors the bride and bridesmaids are wearing
- White chalk (perfect for shoe scuffs on fabric)
- White shoe polish
- Makeup remover and nail polish remover, as well as cotton balls and Q-Tips to clean any makeup or nail polish smudges. To avoid messing up the rest of your nails with nail polish remover, wrap your hand in a plastic baggie while you handle nail polish remover-soaked cotton balls.

If you can access the wedding site before everyone sets up camp, bring a few things to make the experience extraordinary for the bride. A good time to do this might be while the bride is at her hair and makeup appointment. Or, have one of the groomsmen haul this stuff over, since you might be getting your hair done, too!

- Some soothing supplies – a mini-boom-box with relaxing tunes, a scented candle, a mini fan, and a book of quotes can help the bride feel calm and cool if there is any down time, particularly in the hour before the ceremony when nervous tension can set in.
- A small cache of snacks and drinks – crackers are great for settling nervous stomachs and keeping growling at bay. Limit beverages to water or clear drinks in case of spills. Straws are great for keeping lipstick intact, too!

Story box

My sister was the coolest of cucumbers all through the wedding planning process and in the days before the wedding. Suddenly, on her wedding day, she got really nervous before the ceremony. "Crackers," she said to me about half an hour before her walk down the aisle. "I need crackers NOW." Well, we didn't have any on hand, and the nearest store was 20 minutes away. I ran to a house near the church (yes, in my bridesmaid gown) and rang the doorbell. I asked the lovely stranger if he had any crackers for my sister, a nervous bride. Luckily he did and was nice enough to send me on my way with the whole box. When we passed his house on the way to the reception, I made sure to write down his address so the bride could send him a thank-you note.

--Beth Raymond, Maid of Honor extraordinaire

Preparing Your Toast

At some weddings, the Maid of Honor gives a toast along with the Best Man. If the bride hasn't mentioned it by three weeks or so before the wedding, ask her whether she would like you to give a toast. If she is assuming you are giving a toast, you don't want to be caught unprepared as the Best Man says, "And now for the beautiful Maid of Honor's toast!" If she does *not* want you to give a speech, let her know it's ok; you just want to make sure. You might say, "you haven't mentioned it so I thought I'd ask – do you want me to give a toast at the reception? Feel free to say no, I know that you are trying to keep it casual" (or some other disclaimer that will make the bride feel comfortable declining if she doesn't want it).

If you will be delivering a toast, you should prepare it well in advance. Giving a toast is an honor, and you want to make sure it is well thought out and means something to the bride and groom.

You don't have to be a public speaking guru to give a great Maid of Honor toast. As you prepare to write your speech, write down a few things about the bride and her new husband. Think about:

- How did the couple meet?
- How do you know the bride?
- What did you think of the groom when you first met him?
- What are some funny, touching, or significant memories with the bride? With the bride and groom together?

You won't necessarily include all of this information in your toast, but it can be a good way to get started on ideas. When you are writing the toast, be yourself. Don't try to force humor if you are more of a serious, sentimental type. Conversely, if the bride loves your funny bone, let that shine through in your toast. Use natural language. Avoid unfamiliar words, even if you think you have used the word "love" too many times and turn to the thesaurus for alternatives.

What should you say in your toast, you might be wondering? Most Maid of Honor toasts include a story about the bride and groom, a few sentences expressing your happiness about the life the bride and groom are starting together, and well wishes for the future. You can end your toast with a simple, "to the bride and groom!"

Once your toast is written, have a friend look it over and scan for mistakes. You should practice delivering your speech often; alone in front of a mirror, or to a group of friends. You will feel a lot more comfortable on the wedding day if you practice beforehand.

Preparing for the Honeymoon

The bride should prepare for her honeymoon in the week before the wedding. She will need to pack, confirm travel reservations, and remember to hit the bank for travelers checks. Ask the bride when and where she will need her luggage if she is leaving directly from the reception. Find out if there is a locked room where you can keep the luggage during the reception. You also might stash it in the trunk of your car if you are driving to the reception. Plan ahead so the bride doesn't search desperately for it while she and her husband rush to make the flight. You should also keep the clothes she will be traveling in inside a garment bag at the reception site.

Whether the bride and groom leave for the honeymoon the night of the wedding or the next day, they probably will not have time to gather the gifts and drop them off at home. Ask the bride where she wants the gifts to go after the wedding. You might suggest that the wedding party pitch in and load them in one person's car to bring to a designated spot. Clear up these details before the wedding day so that there are no surprises!

Getting Enough Rest

The last, and perhaps most important, is to make sure that you and the bride get enough rest. This won't be as easy as it seems! It will be easy to get caught up in a million details that all seem to need attention right away, and you and the bride could find yourselves awake into all hours of the morning. Of course, this can be an opportunity for some real bonding between you and the bride: staying up, solving problems together, maybe having a glass of wine or two, and reminiscing about good times while you tie bows on 100 wedding favors can bring you and the bride closer. If you must pull an all-nighter to complete a project, make sure there is still time to catch up on lost sleep before the wedding.

Getting enough sleep will make a world of difference on the wedding day. The fresher your minds are, the easier it will be to deal with those last-minute details, crises, and questions. This is one area where your focus should be on yourself and the bride equally. Many brides take the few days prior to their wedding days off from work. So, if the bride stays up until 2 in the morning working on a last-minute project, she will have more of an opportunity to recuperate than you would if you're getting up at 6 a.m. for a full day at work. If the bride calls you in a panic during the late news, spend a few minutes reassuring her that you will be there the next day after work to help her with all the details, but right now you need to get some sleep so that you can be your best for her. You will both benefit from it in the long run.

As you and the bride work on last minute details, it is easy for the bride (and even you) to begin to feel overwhelmed by everything that needs to be accomplished before the wedding. Be prepared for this! No matter how well planned the wedding is, something unexpected will inevitably crop up. Make a list with the bride of other people who you can both call for help in a pinch. Don't forget to enlist the help of the older kids of friends, too: they can fill vases with water, arrange the place cards by table number, and all sorts of other things. Remind the bride that everyone has been itching for a chance to be a part of the action, and she is really doing them a favor. With the help of others, you can get so much done, and have a great time doing it!

Chapter 4   The Bachelorette Party

Bachelorette parties are a great way to gather the girls, celebrate female friendships, and let loose before the wedding. Throwing the bachelorette party is usually the job of the Maid of Honor, however sometimes another bridesmaid, a coworker, a friend, or family member may take the lead. But if no one else steps forward, you should definitely start the planning!

Bachelorette parties can run the gamut from a low-key evening at someone's home to a full-blown night on the town. The most important thing to keep in mind when you are deciding the activities is the bride's wishes. Has she told you since you were teenagers that she did NOT want a wild night on the town? Does she prefer a quiet dinner over a wild night at a bar? Has she always wanted a wild last hurrah? Respect her wishes. It is not nearly as funny as it seems to shock her with something that will overly embarrass her.

That said, it wouldn't be a bachelorette party if she weren't just a smidgen embarrassed. A gift of a silky nightgown can do the trick nicely.

Guest List

The first thing you need to do is get a guest list from the bride. A bachelorette party usually includes the bride's closest friends and family (all female, of course!). It should include only people the bride is totally comfortable with. Most bachelorette parties include about 10-20 guests.

What about the mothers, you bride may ask? It will be an easy decision for some brides: it is either "I wouldn't dream of having it without my mother and future mother-in-law there to share in the fun," or "there is no way on earth my mother, or even worse *his* mother, will be within miles of my bachelorette party." Either way is just fine!

The decision will be more difficult for other brides. She might want them there, but be hesitant about really cutting loose in their presence. There is a very good solution to this dilemma: host a fun dinner, either at home or at a restaurant and invite the mothers. After dinner, just the girls will go for "dessert." Whether "dessert" means tea and crumpets, or a barrage of drinks with wacky names is up to the bride.

Decide whether guests should bring a gift. If they have already attended several showers, it might be a good idea to go in on one very nice gift from the whole gang, such as a classy lingerie set from an upscale store. If 15 guests chip in $5-$10, you can get something really nice. Or, ask guests to bring a gag gift; these are generally far cheaper. If someone has been looking forward to shopping for something for the honeymoon, she can give it to the bride in private.

Bachelorette Party Ideas

A bachelorette party can be a relaxing night for the bride to gather her thoughts and reminisce with friends, or a crazy she-bang. As you decide what kind of party the bride will love best, keep the guests in mind too. Of course the bride's wishes take center stage, but if you are going out, guests will be spending money on food and drinks as well.

Here are a few ideas to satisfy any taste:

1. **The Spa Night** – Designed to help the bride relax while pampering her with facials, pedicures, and more.

First, prepare fresh, healthful appetizers. Fruit and veggie trays, chicken salad, delicate crepes, finger sandwiches, pasta salad, and juices are very appropriate. If you want something more substantial, order gourmet veggie pizzas. Stock your freezer with lots of ice and frozen fruit for smoothies.

Ask each guest to bring their favorite spa supplies – a facial mask, pedicure supplies, massage oils, hair treatments, rich lotions, etc. While the guests apply masks and help each other with pedicures, everyone should take a turn doing their favorite treatment to the bride. Or, hire an aesthetician with all the supplies and know-how (hire one still in training for a better deal) to beautify the whole gang!

Play soft, soothing music at first, and as everyone begins to let loose play funkier tunes to help the party get rolling!

If you are doing a spa night bachelorette party, make sure it is not the night before the wedding. Most facials show maximum results a few days after it is applied. And, if the bride has an allergic reaction to the full body mud mask she used, she will have a chance to let it clear up before the big day!

2. **Night of a Thousand Laughs**

Laughing can be a major stress buster. Gather the gang and head to a comedy club. Or go to a karaoke joint! Most places will have dinner available, and drinks shouldn't be hard to come by either.

3. **Theme party.**

Is the bride into all things southwestern? Throw a party to reflect her tastes. Have an enchilada buffet, a grilling pit, and margaritas. String little chili pepper lights around a friend's garden. No matter what she is into, celebrate her unique tastes!

4. **Fondue festivities.**

Head down to your local fondue restaurant and go nuts! You can also buy fondue pots for a home get-together for $15-$30 each, and they make a great gift to leave behind for the bride. You can concoct all kinds of fun flavors -- place each pot at a different table. Try cheese with bread; chocolate with pound cake, pineapple, brownie, and marshmallows; or surf and turf in a bouillon base (throw your veggies right in there too).

Idea Box

Always have non-alcoholic beverages on hand when the bachelorette party is at home. You never know what might happen – someone may be on the mend from the flu, the bride might not drink as much due to shot nerves, or maybe one of the guests just found out she is carrying a little bundle of joy – but hasn't told anyone yet. Sparkling cider, seltzer, and soda (with cherries and a delicate straw, of course) are all staples of the non-alcoholic bachelorette party!

---

5. The Mystical Soiree

Does on of the bride's friends have a knack with tarot cards or palm reading? Make a mysterious party atmosphere by hanging funky fabric from the center of your ceiling, then pull it back and attach it to the walls so you have a tent-like feel. Light candles, burn incense, and see what the future holds for the bride and her friends! You might even hire a professional, or buy dream interpretation dictionary and designate a dream reader!

6. Garden Party

For a very low-key evening, prepare you or a friend's garden with twinkling lights, soft music, good food, and plenty of patio recliners. Kick it up a notch and rent a hot tub – it can cost as little as $200 for a 4-day rental including all the setup!

7. Getting a little crazier...

If the bride would think that her wedding experience just wouldn't be complete without one last glorious gala with her girlfriends, you might want to make it a little wilder. If you do, make sure there are still a few days before the wedding so the bride won't have to contend with a headache on her big day!

Most bachelorette parties of this variety involve alcohol. You might start with a pub crawl in the hip part of town. Make sure you can walk everywhere, or else rent a limo, bus, or taxis so everyone stays safe. Have one final destination spot in mind to stay put for the last couple hours. Mark the bride as the center of the party by having her wear a wedding veil out on the town! Just not *the* veil she plans to wear at her wedding – you can buy cheap imitations at most party stores. She will get lots of extra attention from other revelers!

The bride will really appreciate her last night with her girlfriends before she ties the knot – with a little planning and lots of laughs, you can make it a truly special day in her life!

Chapter 5   The Wedding Day

All the planning, worrying, excitement, and anticipation have boiled down to this day: The Wedding Day. The bride is going to look to you today to be her right-hand woman, her shelter from the storm, a sounding board for a slew of last-minute concerns and details. Are you up for it? Of course you are!

Getting Ready

If you are with the bride first thing in the morning, make sure she eats breakfast! She might feel nervous and not have much of an appetite, but try to convince her to eat some cereal or fruit. It might be a while before she has an opportunity to eat again. She will love you forever if you keep some snacks handy throughout the morning too – throw a few granola bars or fresh fruit in your purse.

Throughout the day, make sure both you and the bride stay hydrated. Dehydration and hunger are major causes of lightheadedness, dizziness, and feeling faint. If the bride starts feeling any of these things, her nervous meter will likely go off the charts. Try to coax her to snack on little things throughout the morning, and continue to offer her bottled water, especially while you are on the go. Get most of your water in during the earlier part of the morning. Think of it this way: most weddings are scheduled so that pictures take place just after the ceremony, then the wedding party heads off to the reception, where all the guests want to greet the bride and groom, as well as you and the rest of the wedding party. Once the wedding starts, it could be a while before you and the bride have a chance to eat or drink anything.

If the bride has a hair and/or makeup appointment, make sure she gets to it on time and remembers cash for a tip. Button-up shirts are the best attire for these appointments, so that she won't ruin her fabulous new 'do by yanking a shirt over her head.

Use the time during the bride's appointment to relax, de-stress, and center yourself. It will be one of the few moments of the day when you will not be "on." Let her chat with her stylist; it is a great way for her to renew her excitement and temporarily set aside any worries about last-minute details.

Going to the Chapel

After hair and makeup is done, most brides and their maids of honor go to the ceremony site. Many brides start feeling nervous on the ride there. What if the flowers haven't been delivered? What other glitches might I be faced with when I arrive? Is the groom there yet? What am I getting myself into? The best thing you can do for the bride on the way to the ceremony is simply to chat with her, listen to her fears, and try to calm her down. Assure her that all is well, and you are there to help her with any last-minute details. Tell her how happy you are that she has found the love of her life and they are about to start such a wonderful life together. Focus on the positives and the big picture. Try to make her laugh; laughter is one of the best de-stressing devices available.

When you arrive at the ceremony site, tell the bride to take a minute to gather her thoughts and excitement in the car while you scope out the groom's location so they don't see each other. If she is extraordinarily nervous, leave a bridesmaid with her to talk things out. Your duty right now is to scope things out, make sure the groom won't see the bride, and quickly make sure everything is as it should be. If you notice a major problem, the bride will be better off hearing it from your calm and reasoning voice than to see it for herself with no warning. If you haven't already done so, scope out an out-of-sight staging area where the bride and bridesmaids can line up just before the ceremony begins. Try to be quick in doing these things; the less time she has to wait, the better. When you return to the car for the bride, assure her that everything is beautiful and going according to plan, then show her so she can see for herself.

If something *is* going wrong at the ceremony site, tell the bride calmly and gently, have a plan of action, and immediately move on to something exciting or fun to do. Suppose the wrong flowers were delivered: the wedding colors are black and red, and the flowers they sent are bright orange and lime green. Call the florist to clear it up before the bride finds out. Say to the bride, "everything looks great:

the florist sent the wrong truck here, but I've called them and they are on their way with the right ones. They will be here in twenty minutes, so the problem is solved. Let's go get your dress on!" See why it is important to have a list of phone numbers and a cell phone? Crisis averted!

Once you are all inside and getting ready, one of your duties as Maid of Honor is to act as a liaison between the bride, groom, and officiator. When the bride needs to leave the room where she is getting ready, go before her to make sure the groom won't see her. If the officiator needs to talk to the bride to go through last-minute details, it is your job to make sure the bride is dressed (in anything, just not in the process of changing!) and prepared. Once the bride is in her dress, your train-arranging duties have officially begun. Practice a few times if you haven't already. Depending on the length of the train and where the bride needs to go before the wedding, you might need to hold the train up for her so it stays clean. Stay close by in case she needs help!

The bride might be faced with small glitches, as she gets dressed and ready for the ceremony. Have your emergency kit on hand to deal with problems that arise. Again, calm the bride's nerves by focusing on solutions and moving on to something fun as quickly as you can.

As the bride gets ready at the ceremony site, you also need to make sure the bridesmaids are there, getting ready, and know what to do. Have the bridesmaids pitch in if you need to check on three things at once. If there is a flower girl, you or the bride might assign one of the bridesmaids to be her buddy for the morning. She will likely need more attention than you or the bride has time for. It is your responsibility to make sure the flower girl feels comfortable walking down the aisle – spend a minute with her at some point to answer any questions she has, tell her how beautiful she looks, and that she will do a fabulous job. Reassure her again as you are getting in line for the beginning of the ceremony.

The best thing you can do for the bride on the morning before the wedding is to be flexible. There's no way of predicting what might come up, and the more you can be there for the bride, the more she will appreciate your efforts.

Here Comes the Bride...

Time for a walk down the aisle! Just before you leave the dressing room, take a minute with the bride to tell her gorgeous she is, and how smoothly everything is going. Give her a chance to vent any last-minute jitters. This is the final decompression session she will have before facing a crowd of her closest family and friends, and her new husband. Savor the moment!

Make sure not to line up for the ceremony too early. Nothing can build up more tension than a lot of waiting alone. Don't worry, they won't start without the bride! Get the bridesmaids settled into line first, then spend a moment with the bride. If someone is walking her down the aisle, you have a little breather here. Let that person be with the bride right now. You'll see her at the altar!

Proceed down the aisle in the way you practiced at the rehearsal. Your job during the ceremony is to arrange the bride's train, hold her flowers during vows and any other special moments that require her hands to be free, and enjoy your close friend getting married! When arranging the bride's dress, make sure it is smooth and fully displayed. A major reason to arrange the dress is so that it looks good in pictures. Arrange her dress when she has just reached the altar after walking down the aisle, just before the vows when she turns to face her beloved, and any other time she moves enough to disrupt it.

The Maid of Honor sometimes holds the groom's ring during the ceremony until it is needed during the vows. Other times the best man holds onto both rings. If you are designated to hold the groom's ring, keep it safe! You might attach a small velvet jewelry bag to the back of your bouquet, or simply put it on your thumb.

All weddings are different, so there are very few hard and fast rules to define your responsibilities during the ceremony itself. Pay close attention during the rehearsal so you know how you can help. When you have no duties during the ceremony, pay close attention to details that you can recount to her later – brides often miss a lot of the details because they are so swept away in the moment.

At some point, you will be asked to sign the marriage license as a witness to the wedding. It's pretty straightforward, just make sure to be there when they need you for it. You should get more details about this at the rehearsal.

Pictures

Many brides have a photo shoot just after the ceremony to capture group shots of the wedding party and of the bride and groom alone. If you have a purse with you, have the bride's lipstick and powder handy for touch-ups. Talk to the bride in advance to see if there is anything in particular you can do for her during the pictures. You can be most helpful by keeping the wedding party in one place. Aside from a quick restroom break, try to keep the bridesmaids, groomsmen, and any other family of the bride and groom who will be in pictures in one place. If anyone gets antsy, remind them that the sooner you finish pictures, the sooner they can get a snack at the reception!

Bustling the Gown

After pictures, the bride will most likely be ready to bustle her gown. Help her arrange it neatly and comfortably so she doesn't have to worry about it during the reception. Keep an eye on it throughout the reception so you can rearrange it if it comes loose. Be close at hand to help as the bride gets in the car to make sure the dress is all the way in the car before the door is closed.

The Reception

There are a few things that a Maid of Honor traditionally does at the reception. If there is a receiving line either outside the ceremony site or at the reception site, the Maid of Honor generally stands next to the groom in a receiving line. Be gracious, introduce yourself to people you don't know, and keep an eye on the bride in case she needs to be rescued from a talkative third cousin four-times removed who is holding up the line for too long!

Most receptions start with some mingling, during which the bride will probably be busy chatting with guests. You might see if she needs something to drink, but there are no strict guidelines about your duties right now. Enjoy yourself – you deserve it!

The Maid of Honor Toast

If you are giving a toast at the reception, here's your moment to shine. Most toasts happen after drinks have been served and while everyone is seated for the meal. The band or DJ will often announce that toasts will be made, which is your cue to get ready. Take a few deep, relaxing breaths. Everyone is nervous when giving a toast, so you are not alone!

Remember to speak slowly and clearly during your toast. What feels too slow to you probably sounds just right to the guests. At the end of your toast, lift your glass, and take a sip.

The Bouquet Toss

If the bride chooses to toss her bouquet to a crowd of available bachelorettes at the reception, help her corral the crowd to gather. If there is a band or DJ, they will help with this as well. If you are single, set a good example by participating!

Leaving for the Honeymoon

When the festivities are drawing to a close, help the bride change out of her dress. She will likely want to leave pretty soon thereafter, so hang it up for her and make sure it goes to a safe place. Often the bride's mother will take the wedding dress home with her to keep for the bride until she returns from her honeymoon, but if no one steps in, take control yourself! Hang it up and replace any plastic garment coverings. If you bring it home with you, the safest place for it to hang is on the inside of a door that isn't used often, for example a guestroom or spare bathroom. Make sure the bride knows you have it so she doesn't think it is lost!

Enlist the help of other bridesmaids or groomsmen to get the couple's gifts out of the reception site. Load up cars and arrange to drop the gifts off to the couple after the wedding.

Chapter 6   After the Wedding

The wedding day is over, the bride and her new husband are off enjoying their honeymoon, and things have finally settled down. There are just a few more things you can do as a Maid of Honor to help the bride finish up all the last details.

Gifts

The first thing the bride and her groom will likely do after the wedding is open gifts. Some brides choose to open gifts just before her and her husband leave for the honeymoon, others wait until they return. Ask the bride whether she would like you to be there to take notes as she opens gifts. As the bride and groom open gifts, write down:

- Who the gift is from
- What the gift is
- Any particularly special words in the card.

The bride and groom will be able to personalize their thank-you notes to each guest.

Story box

A few days after the bride and groom opened their gifts, I went to the bride's house and helped her address thank-you notes. We recounted stories from the wedding over tea and leftover wedding cake, and had a great time. There were a lot of details the bride had missed, and she enjoyed hearing about how much fun her guests had at the reception. It was also a great chance for me to hear all about her exotic honeymoon in Greece!

--Lisa Peterson, Maid of Honor extraordinaire

Details, Details

Another task the bride might have after the wedding is returning materials to vendors. Some cake vendors require that the bride return the cake plate, for example. The reception site manager might have given the bride a power cord that the band or DJ left behind. Your list of vendors might come in handy to the bride for this purpose.

Many brides choose to have the wedding gown and bouquet preserved. The gown can usually wait until after the bride returns from her honeymoon. Volunteer to drop it off while the bride honeymoons.

Ask the bride what you can do to help after the wedding. She will likely have more time now to handle many details herself, but certain things might need to be done while she is out of town.

As Time Goes By

Once all the post-wedding details are wrapped up, it's back to normal. Congratulations, you have done well for the bride. She could not have done it without you, and your friendship is all the stronger for it. Do something special for yourself: you deserve it!

Printed in Great Britain
by Amazon